Easy-to-Us

SERMON OUTLINES ON COMFORT AND ASSURANCE

Charles R. Wood

kregel
PUBLICATIONS

Grand Rapids, MI 49501

Sermon Outlines on Comfort and Assurance by Charles R. Wood.

Copyright © 1994 by Charles R. Wood.

Published in 1994 by Kregel Publications, a division of Kregel, Inc., P.O. Box 2607, Grand Rapids, MI 49501. Kregel Publications provides trusted, biblical publications for Christian growth and service. Your comments and suggestions are valued.

Cover Design: Alan G. Hartman

Library of Congress Cataloging-in-Publication Data
Wood, Charles R. (Charles Robert), 1933–
    Sermon outlines on comfort and assurance / Charles R. Wood.
        p.   cm. (Easy-to-use sermon outline series)
    Includes index.
    1. Assurance (Theology)—Sermons—Outlines, syllabi,
etc. 2. Consolation—Sermons—Outlines, syllabi, etc.
3. Sermons, American—Outlines, syllabi, etc. 4. Baptists—
Sermons—Outlines, syllabi, etc. I. Title. II. Series: Wood,
Charles R. (Charles Robert), 1933– Easy-to-use sermon
outline series.
BT785.W59   1994   251'.02—dc20   93-49093
                                                    CIP

ISBN 0-8254-4059-9 (paperback)

2 3 4 5 Printing / Year 98

Printed in the United States of America

Contents

List of Scripture Texts

Introduction

In a time of great national and international upheaval, the average Christian is often confused, discouraged, and "stressed-out." Just meeting the demands of everyday living sometimes becomes more than many can handle.

Fortunately, the Word of God was written for people like us who lived in times like ours. Along with the Bible's commandments and instruction are specific promises and numerous stories of real people who endured difficult times and emerged triumphant because of God's help and sustaining grace.

Unfortunately, the evangelical pulpit has often failed to sense the actual needs of God's people, and it has tended to emphasize admonition and exhortation to the exclusion of encouragement. This need not be the case, and it ought not to be so. For this reason, then, I have set out to restore a biblical balance in my own preaching by including frequent messages of comfort, hope, and assurance. The sermons contained in this volume have all been preached from the pulpit of Grace Baptist Church in South Bend, Indiana, a congregation made up of people that are typically found in any Bible-believing church.

I encourage you to carefully study the relevant Scripture passages included with each sermon prior to preaching these messages in order to help flesh out the "bare bones" of these outlines. Such study will also enable the skillful preacher to craft more than one sermon from many of these messages.

In a day of broken hearts, struggling spirits, and confused consciences, may our gracious God be pleased to use these sermons in multiplied ways in the lives of other preachers and congregations and thus provide comfort and assurance for God's people. May the Holy Spirit who empowered their original preparation also guide their representation to usefulness in His service.

CHARLES R. WOOD

The Sin of Discouragement
Numbers 32:1–9

Introduction:

God gave His people one of worst condemnations possible: aimless wandering leading to ultimate death. It must have been terrible sin which cause this. No, it was simply unbelief causing disobedience.

I.   **The Incident at the Edge of the Jordan**
   A. The spies discouraged Israel thus encouraging disobedience.
   B. They did it by:
      1. Negativity.
      2. Sharing wrong estimates.
      3. Contradicting God.
   C. Reuben, Gad, half Manasseh were in danger of same sin in different form—discouraging Israel by:
      1. Not participating.
      2. Doing nothing.

II. **The New Testament Parallel**
   A. Matthew 18:6
   B. Offending little ones.
      1. Discouraging the immature.
      2. It is a serious matter.

III. **The Modern Applications**
   A. We have an incorrect view of the seriousness of sin.
      1. What we call serious: adultery, immorality, theft, dishonesty, rebellion.
      2. Most serious: unbelief, disobedience.
   B. We all have a sphere of influence.
      1. Some of which evident.
      2. Some of which we may not be aware.
   C. We stand in danger of discouraging others, especially those we influence.
      1. Negativity.
      2. Sharing wrong estimates.
      3. Contradicting God.
      4. Failing to participate.
      5. Doing nothing.

D. Special danger seems to attract to:
   1. Those who influence young people and Christians.
   2. Those who were once active, vital, involved, and now.
   3. Those who do nothing.

Conclusion:

Are you discouraging others? Resolve not to discourage by words, actions, or failing to act.

Up from the Dumpster

Nehemiah 4

Introduction:
It can strike anyone, and it does strike most. It does not respect persons, affecting leaders and followers alike. It saps energy, consumes strength, distorts vision, and can even cause physical ailments. What is it? Discouragement!

I. **The Causes of Discouragement**
   A. Difficult circumstances.
   B. Opposition (vv. 1–2).
      1. Whole book of Nehemiah is a story of this.
      2. More are added in this time.
   C. Ridicule (v. 3)—weight of a fox will break down what they have built.
   D. Overwhelming problems (v. 10).
   E. Lack of discernible progress (v. 6)—"We've worked this hard and only come this far?"
   F. Fear of the unknown (v. 11)—Undefined threats that included murder.
   G. Criticism (v. 2).
   H. Uncertainty regarding the future (v. 12)—no matter where you turn, there will be trouble, and the opposition is sure to succeed.
   I. Undermining by those who should support (v. 12)—Fears of friends can be worse than threats of enemies.
   J. Boredom—the newness had worn off the task.

II. **The Symptoms of Discouragement**
   A. Loss of strength (v. 10).
      1. Strength of bearers were undermined.
      2. They are staggering, tottering from exhaustion.
      3. Everyone is simply "out of gas."
   B. Loss of vision (v. 10).
      1. "Yet" there is much rubbish.
      2. They were looking at the rubble rather than the wall.
      3. They could no longer envision completed wall.
   C. Loss of confidence (10).
      1. We are not able to do the job.
      2. The people had a heart for the work.
      3. The people have now lost heart (motivation).

D. Loss of security (v. 11).
   1. No longer sure or secure in anything.
   2. A sense of loose-endedness had taken over.
   3. They were ready to retreat and quit the job.

III. The Cure for Discouragement
   A. Reaffirm God (vv. 4–6, 14).
      1. Recall who God is.
      2. Recall the things God has said (promises).
      3. Recall the things God has done.
   B. Re-focus efforts (v. 13).
      1. Briefly stopped the work (sometimes need to do this).
      2. Reorganized, stressing families.
   C. Recommit efforts (vv. 14–17).
      1. Return to the task.
      2. Be on guard—wary and aware.
      3. WORK.
   D. Renew determination (vv. 19–20).
      1. Fight if necessary.
      2. Determine to keep on going no matter what.
   E. Review focus (vv. 21–23).
      1. Get your focus off yourself.
      2. Become involved in others.
      3. Get lost again in the cause.

Conclusion:

Discouragement is one of Satan's primary weapons. Nehemiah gives us the pattern for overcoming this scourge: reaffirm God, re-focus efforts, recommit to the task, renew determination, review focus. Will you take the help proffered?

Running Over

Psalm 23:5

Introduction:

In comparison to the rest of the world, all of us have cups that are running over. Spurgeon said, "Not only have I enough, but more than enough; I possess not only all that I am capable of containing, but I inherit an excess of joy, a redundancy of blessing, an extravagance of favor, a prodigality of love."

I. **Some cups don't run over.**
    A. Because they are taken to the wrong source for filling.
        1. A Christian can't get filled at the world's leaky cistern.
        2. There are things that will never cause a cup to run over:
            a. Wealth
            b. Pleasure
            c. Fame
    B. Because those who own them suffer from the disease of discontent.
        1. A discontented man dooms himself to the worst poverty of all—poverty of spirit.
        2. The discontented will always be discontent.
    C. Because there is envy of others.
        1. "There are vices peculiar to the rich, but this is one of the faults of poverty."
        2. Romans 12:15 shows the way to an overflowing cup—make everything yours.
    D. Because of lack of faith.
        1. Much of what we receive comes by faith.
        2. Man without faith will seldom overflow.
    E. Because of unbelief.

II. **Some cups do run over.**
    A. Because having Christ, we have in Him all things.
        1. "Between here and heaven there is nothing we shall want but that God has already supplied."
        2. Romans 8:32 explains perfectly.
        3. God's blessings are like gift wrapping.
    B. Because the infinite God Himself is ours.
    C. Because abundant blessings are promised to us.
    D. Because we receive more than we ever pray for.
    E. Because we surely receive more than we actually deserve.

III. **If your cup is overflowing . . .**
   A. Stop to worship Him Who has filled your cup.
   B. Pray that the Lord will make the overflow even larger.
      1. No problem with that prayer if overflow used wisely.
      2. "There is too much narrowness in the largest-hearted man."
   C. Keep the cup where it is.
      1. Don't take it from under the spring.
      2. Don't take credit for producing what has come through His blessings.
      3. "Prosperity has spoiled many more than poverty."
   D. Make sure that others share in the overflow.
      1. "If God fills us, it is that we may bless others."
      2. The Bible teaches that to withhold is to impoverish; to scatter is to increase.
   E. Concentrate on the fullness of the One by Whom your cup is filled.

Conclusion:

Can you sing, "My cup is full and running over?" If you can't, what's wrong? Are you seeking from the wrong source, suffering from general discontent, envious of what others have, or lacking in faith? Or are you an unbeliever? Be sure to keep your cup under the flow of His blessing.

Delight Thyself in the Lord

Psalm 37:4

Introduction:
Have you ever been let down by someone? Found something to be other than it appeared? Lost interest in something that was once special? Failed to find satisfaction where you expected it? Found that no matter how much you had it wasn't enough? Had a sense of unfulfillment, restlessness, dissatisfaction?

I.   **A Required Attitude**
    A. "Delight"
        1. Initial meaning: soft, pliable, luxuriate
        2. To derive great joy or pleasure from, to be highly pleased.
        3. "Luxuriate in God."
    B. "Thyself"
        1. An action.
        2. Some decision of the will is necessary.
        3. This is something one chooses to do.
    C. "In the Lord"
        1. The Lord becomes the object of delight, etc.
        2. "In"—with, beside, by, in the presence of, before.
        3. "Make the Lord the object of your delight" (a dozen qualities to delight in: His presence, person, power, provision, patience, peace, perfections, permanence, purposes, promises, principles, protection, purity).
    D. How do we delight ourselves in the Lord?
        1. Through studying Him.
        2. Through sensing Him and His presence.
        3. Through seeking His face.
        4. Through submission to His ways.
        5. Through surrender to His will.

II. **A Relational Aspect**
    A. Note the order of the verse.
        1. "Delight thyself in the Lord."
        2. As a result, "He shall give thee the desires . . ."
    B. The gift is a result of the delighting.
        1. We are not to delight because of His gifts.
        2. We are to delight regardless of any gifts.
    C. Receiving the desires of one's heart is dangerous without delight in the Lord (would create bedlam if everyone did).

III. A Recorded Assurance
A. "He shall give Thee"
1. This is clearly a promise.
2. Note the source—even though through others.
3. "Give"—freest Hebrew word available.
B. "The desires of thine heart"
1. The question:
   a. What you want.
   b. Make you want what you should.
2. A word of petition—He will give you that which you desire of Him.
3. This is conditioned by delighting in Him.
   a. Will want what He would want.
   b. Will not want what He wouldn't want.
4. There are specific requirements for answered prayer—thus this is not *carte blanche*.

Conclusion:
We live in a world that is seldom satisfied, and dissatisfaction takes its toll in stress. Delighting in the Lord is a stress reliever, and such delight is also productive: delight determines desires, delight defines desires, delight directs desires, delight dissolves desires. "Delight thyself also in the Lord!" Are you doing so?

God Is Worth Waiting For

Psalm 37:7

Introduction:

There are various kinds of stress: that caused by prosperity of wicked, that caused by need and inadequacy, that caused by life's fleeting satisfactions, and that caused by the difficulties of living the Christian life. But there is still another: the stress caused by the struggle with the unexplainable things of life.

I. **An Argument**
   A. There are many things in life we can't explain.
      1. Some we feel acute need to explain.
      2. Being a Christian can make this worse.
   B. We tend to argue with God over these things.
      1. Jacob—Genesis 42:36
      2. Elijah—1 Kings 19:4
      3. Jonah—Jonah 4:9
   C. Such arguments are strong stress producers.

II. **An Antidote**
   A. "Rest in the Lord."
      1. Common theme in Psalms, but different here.
      2. Comes from word that means "dumb."
      3. "Be silent toward the Lord."
   B. "Wait patiently for Him."
      1. Has idea of finding refreshment in repose.
      2. "Wait quietly until you hear from Him."
      3. These two things are in combination.
   C. Produces difficult requirement.
      1. "The hardest thing a Christian ever has to do is nothing; the second hardest is to wait."
      2. "A silent tongue shows a wise head and a holy heart."
      3. "Time is nothing to Him; let it be nothing to thee."

III. **An Application**
   A. Psalmist brings in specific example of what he means here.
      1. Don't get upset over something hard to understand.
      2. Best to reverse clauses here: man who brings wicked devices to pass yet prospers in his way.
   B. Reason for example.
      1. In accord with theme of chapter.
      2. Common to our experience.

IV. An Assurance

A. When faced with the inexplicable:
   1. Bring it before the Lord.
   2. Leave it before the Lord.
   3. Leave it up to the Lord.
B. You will be helped if you can realize:
   1. God has a plan for every situation.
   2. God knows what He is doing.
   3. God's timing, of necessity, is perfect.
C. Note of caution:
   1. If things are not left with and up to Him, more stress can be created.
   2. Strong element of submission is called forth here.

Conclusion:

Things we can't understand and control can create stress. We must remember, "There is more of the love of God in your defeats than there is in the successes of the wicked." "Don't criticize the drama if you leave before it is completed."

In God's Waiting Room

Psalm 37:34

Introduction:

The dictionary says, "to wait is to stay in one place, to remain still until someone comes or something happens." We hate waiting in lines, in restaurants, on the mail, etc. We have many problems in the spiritual realm where God operates in a different relationship to time.

I.   **The Principle: "Wait on the Lord and keep His way."**
  A. Biblical meaning
     1. To wait for God's proper time.
     2. To listen quietly for God's voice.
     3. To refuse to act until sure of God's purpose.
  B. Biblical portraits
     1. Psalm 104:27
        a. Has to do with animals and creation.
        b. Stresses submission.
     2. Psalm 123:2
        a. Has to do with servants and masters.
        b. Stresses submission.
  C. Biblical illustrations
     1. Abraham waiting for Isaac.
     2. Jacob waiting for Rachel.
     3. Joseph waiting for vindication.
     4. Moses waiting for leadership.
     5. Job waiting for restoration.
     6. David waiting for the kingdom.
     7. Anna/Simeon waiting for fulfillment.
     8. Paul waiting for ministry and freedom.

II. **The Problem**
  A. Human tendencies
     1. Most dislike waiting.
     2. Our day is particularly oriented toward immediacy.
     3. Tend to take things into our own hands.
  B. Human tendency exposed
     1. Middle East problem very pressing right now.
     2. Comes as result of Abraham's failure to wait on God.
     3. No way to see danger any more clearly.

C. Dual difficulty involved
   1. It is hard to wait on God
   2. It is even more difficult to know when we should wait on God and when we should act.

III. The Precepts
A. Practical pointers
   1. It's always right to do right (it is never right to do what it is not right to do).
   2. You don't have to make a decision until you have to make a decision.
   3. When you don't know what to do, don't do anything until you do know what to do (when you don't know what to do, do what you already know to do until you do know what else to do).
B. Biblical confirmation
   1. Hebrews 10:36
   2. Galatians 6:9; 2 Thessalonians 3:13
C. Necessary qualities
   1. Humilty
   2. Patience
   3. Submission
   4. Belief, trust, faith

Conclusion:
Waiting is one of the two hardest things we have to do (nothing is the other). God has His timetable; we do well to conform to it. "He that truly trusts in God will never step out of the way that is right, no matter how long he may be called upon to wait."

Heads Up

Psalm 42, 43

Introduction:

These two Psalms were orginally either one or designed to go together. We don't know if they were written by or for David, but they contain a clear expression of David's type of thinking.

I. **David's Anguish**
    A. Likely during Absalom's rebellion.
        1. Son turned again him.
        2. Knew it was his own fault.
    B. Separated from familiar contacts.
    C. Strong language of upset (humanly, had good reason for upset).

II. **David's Argument**
    A. He is actually talking to himself here.
    B. What he is saying.
        1. Two sides to discouraging events.
        2. We generally look on dark side.
        3. Looking thus is voluntary—"why wilt thou deject thyself?"
        4. Doing so is really wrong, and we are guilty for so doing.
        5. It is the duty of God's people to look on the other side.
    C. He actually reproves himself.

III. **David's Assurance**
    A. Soul should hope in God.
    B. Reasons for such hope.
        1. "I will yet get to acknowledge the help of His countenance."
        2. "I will yet see Him help my countenance."
            a. He will clear it up.
            b. He will enlighten it.
        3. "I shall yet acknowledge Him as my God."
            a. Sorrowful with such a God?
            b. Sorrowful within when it can be emptied out to Him?
            c. Cast down and gloomy with such an one in Whom to hope?

C. Produces strong arguments against the upset that had siezed him.

Conclusion:

It is common to our experience to have trials and even anguish and to be internally cast down. David has some words for us at those times. We choose to be, we don't need to be, and we are wrong in so being. David has the answer for us. Look to God for light and wait upon God for solutions. HEADS UP!!!

How to Handle an Upset

Psalm 42:5, 11; 43:5

Introduction:

Some people use rolaids, others tums, some mylanta, still others bicarbonate of soda. Everyone has an answer to an upset stomach. But what do you do about other upsets, emotional and spiritual? Here's an answer for you in a time of trouble.

I. **There Are Two Questions to Ask Yourself**
   A. "Why art thou cast down [bowed down], O my soul?"
      1. Identify cause of upset—what really has you upset?
      2. Sometimes cause vague or not what appears on surface.
   B. "Why art thou disquieted within me?" (Why dost thou make thy moan over me?)
      1. Is the cause worth the upset?
      2. Should I be upset? ("Sorrow of heart springs from unbelief rather than from the greatness of the evils faced.")
      3. Is the upset proportional to the cause?
      4. What about God?

II. **There Is a Commitment to Make to Yourself**—"Hope thou in God"
   A. Hope involves expectantly waiting for someone/thing—God ("There is need of patience where there is ground for hope.")
   B. Hope is based on God's revelation of Himself.
      1. His statements
      2. His performance (for self and others)
      3. His character
   C. Hope is a prophet of future benefits.
      1. It points to the potential of coming good.
      2. Who would have predicted the outcome of Jonah, Nebuchadnezzar, Joseph, Job, Lazarus?
      3. "God never did, will, can desert the soul that leans on Him."
   D. Hope is exclusive.
      1. It is a matter of "members only."
      2. Membership, however, is open to all.
   E. Hope is essential for balanced living—"Like the highest form of courage, it is a refusal to be borne down and cowed and depressed by evil—a refusal to indulge in

the melancholy pleasure of looking and dwelling on the dark side of things."

III. **There Is an Assurance to Take for Yourself**
   A. "I shall yet praise Him."
      1. Things will happen which will call forth my praise.
      2. There are yet good things ahead—even in the very realm of my present trouble.
   B. The reasons for my praise.
      1. "The help of His countenance"—He will cause His face to shine.
      2. "The health of my countenance" (the salvation of my face)—He will give me cause to smile again no matter what.
      3. "My God."
      4. The confidence it gives—hope in God gives rest.

Conclusion:
   When your stomach is upset, reach for your favorite antacid. When your emotions and spirit are upset, reach for the Word of God and ask yourself those questions: What am I upset about? Should I really be upset about it? Commit yourself to trust in God. Take the assurance offered—I shall YET praise Him.

A Comforting Word in a Chaotic World

Psalm 46

Introduction:
We all face so much turbulence: loss of loved ones, marriage break-ups, unemployment, loss of a friendship, a move, business problems, financial pressure, etc. The Bible has a comforting word for such chaotic times, and we need to turn to its truth frequently.

I.   **The Statement of the Psalm** (vv. 1–3)
    A. The reality—"We will not fear."
       1. Even though:
          a. The earth be removed (destroyed).
          b. The mountains be carried into the sea (most established things on earth be carried away).
          c. The seas roil and be turbulent (tidal waves).
          d. The mountains swell and shake (volcanic eruptions).
       2. We will not fear, no matter how bad things get— even if the natural order is overturned.
    B. The reasons—because God is:
       1. Our refuge—place of protection (passive).
       2. Our strength—source of strength (also passive).
       3. Our help—the One Who comes to our aid (active).
          a. Very—exceedingly.
          b. Present—proved, found out to be.
          c. In time of trouble—anything that comes.
    C. The result—we need not fear no matter what comes, from the very most to the very least.

II. **The Stresses of the Psalm** (vv. 4–7)
    A. His protection (v. 4).
       1. Picture of peace and calm.
       2. Figurative—speaks of God's dwelling on earth.
    B. His presence (v. 5).
       1. God is in the midst of her—so long as God is in a place, there is no need to fear.
       2. Thus she shall not be moved.
       3. God shall help her—move to meet her need.
       4. Right early—at the turning of the day, the first appropriate moment (if His help has not yet come, it is not yet the proper moment for it to come).

C. His power (v. 6)—tied to historical setting.
   1. Heathen raged—turmoil without.
   2. Kingdoms were moved—men in uproar.
   3. He uttered His voice—all He had to do was speak.
   4. The earth melted—all was still before His word.
D. His promise (v. 7)
   1. The Lord of Hosts—mighty marshal of armies of heaven.
   2. The God of Jacob—concerned with single wanderer.

III. The Significance of the Psalm (vv. 8–11)
A. Invitation (v. 8).
   1. Come behold what God hath done.
   2. Overthrow of men and nations.
   3. Identifications (v. 9).
   4. He makes wars to cease.
   5. He breaketh bow, cutteth spear—renders all human weapons ineffectual.
   6. Burneth chariots—actually destroys weapons.
B. Implications (vv. 10–11).
   1. "Be still"—Hebrews: let your hand sink down, be calm, restful, confident. Let the matter rest with God; don't raise your hand to it.
   2. "And know that I am God"—see the evidence and believe the fact and all it means.
   3. "I will be exalted"—rest assured that I will show myself strong in behalf of my people.

Conclusion:
The statement: we will not fear because God is our refuge and strength. The stresses: God's protection, presence, power, and promises are all ours. The significance: Relax! I am God, and I will be exalted. "Let the worst come to the worst. A child of God need never give way to mistrust. Since God is faithful, there can be no danger to His cause or to His people."

The Lord Is Merciful

Psalm 103:8–12, 17–18

Introduction:
"The Lord is merciful and gracious." Mercy is not getting what one deserves. Grace is getting what one does not deserve. Concentrate on God's mercy!

I. **God has mercy adequate for your needs.**
   A. "Plenteous in mercy" (v. 8).
      1. Abundant, overflowing
      2. Contrasts with verse 6—God more likely to show mercy than to practice judgment.
   B. Comparison (v. 11).
      1. Heaven/earth comparison designed to express infinity.
      2. God's mercy indescribable, incomprehensible.
   C. Express—were it not for:
      1. Sparing mercy, we would all go to hell.
      2. Inviting mercy, none would ever hear the Gospel.
      3. Saving mercy, none would have sinner's prayer answered.
      4. Upholding mercy, none would be able to live Christian life.
      5. Consoling mercy, all would be swallowed up by grief.
      6. Infinite mercy, all would be cut off from the earth.
      7. Everlasting mercy—none would ever get to heaven.

II. **God shows His mercy to you in many ways.**
   A. In regard to His anger.
      1. "Slow to anger" (v. 8).
      2. "He will not always chide" (v. 9).
      3. "Neither will He keep His anger forever" (v. 9).
   B. In regard to your sins.
      1. "He hath not dealt with us after our sins" (v. 10).
         a. He does not give us what we deserve.
         b. He can't deal with our sins because He has already dealt with them.
      2. "Nor rewarded us according to our iniquities" (v. 10).
         a. It is a statement of fact.
         b. Beware of over-judgmental view of God.
      3. "As far as the east is from the west . . ." (v. 12).

        a. Obviously meant to be figure of speech for infinity.
        b. Once confessed, sin is absolutely put away.
        c. If you are carrying a load of guilt, it is your own fault.

III. God's mercy calls forth a response from you.
    A. "... His mercy toward them that fear Him" (v. 11).
        1. Everyone knows something of His mercy.
        2. The mercy described here is primarily for His people.
    B. "The mercy of the Lord is from everlasting ..." (v. 17).
        1. His mercy transcends time as well as space.
        2. It is conditional.
            a. Upon them that fear Him.
            b. His righteousness to children's children.
    C. It is conditional even among those that love Him (v. 18).
        1. Those who live within His covenant.
        2. Those who keep His commandments.
            a. Important not to presume on the mercy of God.
            b. Point of remembering His commandments is to do them.

Conclusion:
There is more of God's mercy than all that has been used. God's mercy shows in very practical ways, and it challenges us. It is most bestowed where there is most wrong. It is most beneficial where there is obedience.

A Pattern in Problems

Psalm 143

Introduction:

Speaking from very strong emotions, David provides an example for us of how to handle adversity and overwhelming trials in our lives.

I. **David's Problem** (v. 3)
   - A. Not sure of specific situation (either Saul or Absalom).
   - B. It is a graphic description.
     1. Enemy has persecuted my *soul*.
     2. Enemy has smitten my life down to the ground.
     3. Enemy has made me dwell in darkness like death.
   - C. Comprehensive phrases describing overwhelming trouble.

II. **David's Predicament** (vv. 4, 7)
   - A. Therefore—as a result of the trouble I face.
   - B. Graphic description
     1. My spirit overwhelmed in the midst of me.
     2. My heart feels abandoned in the midst of me.
     3. My spirit faileth—faces complete failure.
   - C. Comprehensive terms for being overwhelmed (perplexed, afflicted, lonely, overturned).

III. **David's Procedure** (vv. 1, 2, 5, 6, 7, 9, 11)
   - A. Prayer
     1. Content: Deliver me from mine enemies (v. 9).
     2. Condition: "Wanted audience at the mercy-seat but not at the judgment seat" (v. 2).
     3. Concentration: wanted immediate help (v. 7).
     4. Considered: Based all on the character and will of God (vv. 1, 11).
   - B. Desire
     1. Sought to meet the Lord in it (v. 6).
     2. Wanted to experience God in the trial.
   - C. Ordered thinking
     1. Put mind in gear as well as emotions (v. 5).
     2. Dealt with three things in time of trouble:
        - a. Memory
        - b. Meditation
        - c. Musing

IV. **David's Purpose** (vv. 8, 10)
   A. He wanted certain things as a result of the experience.
   B. Note the specific requests.
      1. Cause me to hear—give me encouragement.
      2. Cause me to know—guidance and direction.
      3. Teach me—show me the path of obedience.
      4. Lead me—make me to live as one upright.
   C. The will of God revealed in the Word of God is our rule or our compass; the Spirit of God is the wind that blows us on our course.

V. **David's Persuasion** (v. 12)
   A. Actually statements, not requests.
   B. The nature of his assurance.
      1. God will in mercy dispose of his enemies.
      2. God will deal with those who afflict his soul.
   C. The basis of his assurance is that he is God's servant.

Conclusion:
David wanted God's help, even wanted out of his trials, but he also wanted them put to a positive use in his life. Are you in trouble? Almost overwhelmed? Look at the example of David.

The Day of Adversity
Proverbs 24:10

Introduction:
"When the going gets tough . . ." Someone has suggested, "get going, all right—out the door." It is better to say, when the going gets tough, the tough *keep* going." Solomon has a principle to go by on this subject.

I. **The Time**—In the day of adversity.
   A. Aspects:
      1. When things go wrong.
      2. When they go other than as expected.
      3. Whey they go other than as planned.
      4. When they go other than as desired.
   B. Areas:
      1. Physical
      2. Financial
      3. Emotional—distracting problems
      4. Relational
      5. Situational

II. **The Tendency**—If thou faint.
   A. Not wrong to feel or suffer under.
      1. Many biblical examples.
      2. Part of our humanity.
   B. The many ways of fainting.
      1. Yielding to temptation.
      2. Discouragement/despair.
      3. Compromising.
      4. Choosing to do wrong.
      5. Succumbing to anxiety.
      6. Panicking and running.
      7. Complaining.
      8. Using unlawful means to escape.
      9. Quitting.

III. **The Truth**—Thy strength is small.
   A. Adversity is relative (both in its intensity and its effects).
   B. God is equal to every adversity.
   C. Adversity doesn't build character; it reveals it.
   D. Survival in adversity makes future survival more likely.
   E. Character determines survival.

F. The character that survives adversity is built in the routine of life.
    1. Doing right.
    2. Thinking right.
    3. Exposure to the Word (this is what Ephesians 6:10-18 is all about).
    4. Developing faith.

Conclusion:
"School of hard knocks" has effect of revealing character. It is too late to develop it when the trouble has come. What are you doing now to develop character against the day of adversity?

A Sermon for Myself

Isaiah 26:3

Introduction:

Sometimes those who preach need to hear their own messages. God spoke to the heart of the one who preached this message before it was ever preached.

I. **You can have perfect peace.**
   A. An absence of all strife.
      1. Look up—no fiery wrath.
      2. Look down—no hell to threaten.
      3. Look back—no guilt worth anything.
      4. Look around—all things work for good.
      5. Look ahead—glory shines on the way.
      6. Look out—at peace with the world.
      7. Look in—peace that passeth understanding.
   B. A quiet that reigns over all things.
   C. The removal of every cause of inner fear.
   D. The presence of great blessings.
      1. Peace between the soul and heaven.
      2. Fellowship with all the saints.
   E. Real rest in the soul.
      1. Resignation to the Divine will.
      2. Absolute confidence in God.
      3. Blessed contentment.
   F. Freedom from all despondency.
   G. Keeping from rashness—we can wait God's timing in deliverance.

II. **You can only get this peace from God.**
   A. He operates on the mind in trial.
      1. The Creator knows how to control it.
      2. Sometimes does so specially.
   B. He usually operates by:
      1. Reminding us of what Christ has done.
      2. Turning us to the Word of God.
   C. He orders His providence for us.
      1. Providence matches circumstance.
      2. Either gives rest or extra strength.

III. **You can only gain this peace one way.**
   A. Stay the whole of your being on God.
      1. Your thoughts—beware the vagabond.

    2. Your imagination.
    3. Your desires.
  B. What does it mean to stay.
    1. Just stop with God.
    2. Accept His upholding.
  C. The object so important—God.

IV. Why is this peace sure for you—faith ("Because he trusteth in Thee").
  A. Faith creates and nourishes peace.
  B. Faith is rewarded by peace.
  C. Faith proclaims herself through peace.

Conclusion:

Do you know this peace? Why not? It is designed for you, and you can and should have it.

Good Cause for Comfort
Isaiah 40

Introduction:
God says, "Isaiah, comfort my people." This chapter points out seven bases for that comfort. "Comfort ye my people. . . ."

I. **Because Their Captivity Is Ended** (v. 2)
    A. Specific reference to return from Assyria and Babylonian captivities.
    B. Readily applies to redeemed—captivity ended.

II. **Because Glory of the Lord Shall Be Revealed** (vv. 3–5)
    A. Applied in New Testament to ministry of John the Baptist.
    B. We can take comfort: the glory of the Lord has been revealed.

III. **Because the Word of the Lord Endures** (vv. 6–8)
    A. All else is transitory.
        1. Especially man—he is like grass.
        2. Also nature—the grass passes also.
    B. The Word of God is eternal—it will stand and it will withstand.

IV. **Because of His Tender, Loving Care** (vv. 9–11)
    A. He is compared to a shepherd.
    B. Relationship is compared to that between shepherd and flock.

V. **Because God Is Surpassingly Great** (vv. 12–17)
    A. He is great in creation (v. 12).
    B. He is great in wisdom (vv. 13–14).
    C. He is great in providence (vv. 15, 17).
    D. He is greater than man's religions (v. 16).

VI. **Because He Is Sovereign Over All** (vv. 18–26)
    A. Over all other gods (vv. 18–20).
    B. Over the natural world (vv. 21–22).
    C. Over humanity (vv. 23–24).
    D. Over everything (vv. 25–26).

VII. Because He Ministers to His Own People (vv. 27–31)
   A. His people never "out of sight, out of mind."
   B. He shares with His own people all that He is in and of Himself.

Conclusion:
There is good cause for comfort: Our captivity is ended, the glory of the Lord has been revealed, we have an enduring Word, He provides us tender, loving care, He is surpassingly great, He is absolutely sovereign, and He specially ministers to His own people. If you are not finding comfort, it is likely because you are "stiff-kneed."

Forgiveness

Psalm 51

Introduction:
There are so many problems with sin and its consequences. We need to take a new look at the subject.

I.   Sin Problems
   A. The Christian and guilt.
   B. Lack of consistent victory.
   C. Questions/questionable areas.

II. Society's Confusion
   A. Sin is not serious.
   B. All sorts of things are not sin.

III. Principles in Passage
   A. He made no attempt to cover.
   B. He made no attempt to rationalize.
   C. He saw sin as "in God's sight."
   D. He saw sin as against God.
   E. He saw only answer in God.

Conclusion:
Do you want help in living the Christian life? Why not begin by getting a new view of sin?

God Gives Wings

Isaiah 40:27–31

Introduction:

This familiar passage actually begins at verse 27, and it is full of encouragement for God's people.

I. **A Common Problem** (v. 27)
   A. The question of the prophet.
      1. "Hidden"—sense of unknown, neglected.
      2. "Judgment"—case, suit.
      3. A skeptical despondency as to the fulfillment of God's promises.
   B. Familiar to personal experience.
      1. We suffer, and God seems indifferent.
      2. We see injustice, and God does not right it.
      3. Others hear a message; our heavens are quiet.
      4. Others get answers; we get none.
   C. Problem—we take weaknesses in ourselves and project them on God: "God has forgotten us; He has passed us by; our wrongs and sufferings are disregarded by Him as if hidden from Him."

II. **A Correcting Picture** (v. 28)
   A. Prophet appeals to their intelligence.
      1. Gets attention away from emotion, our usual focus in difficult times.
      2. Complaining Israel is bidden to stay itself upon God.
   B. Prophet emphasizes the attributes of God.
      1. He is everlasting ("beyond the vanishing point").
      2. He is creator—implies providence; if He created it, surely He will sustain it.
      3. He has no infirmities—God is wholly free from whatever is weak in man.
      4. He is unsearchable—unfathomable intelligence; a wise purpose in each providence.
   C. Prophet reminds them of the character and the purposes of God: loving belief will relieve us of a load of care.

III. **A Consummate Provision** (vv. 29–31)
   A. Weakness is to be expected (v. 30)
      1. "Even the youths...even the young men."
      2. "Youths"—those of an age to be drafted into military service.

B. Provision is made (v. 29)
   1. God has ways of reviving weakness and restoring faith.
   2. The fact that it is "increased" means that there is something there to begin with.
   3. The insufficiency of human strength and the adequacy of the divine is shown.
C. Power is provided beyond provision.
   1. God makes special provision.
      a. Renews strength.
      b. Causes us to "raise the pinion."
      c. Provides for every area of life.
   2. God can and does provide.
      a. Resistance
      b. Endurance
      c. Ability to be steadfast in holiness.
      d. Joy
      e. Faithful utterance
      f. Perseverence in good works.
   3. The secret lies in waiting on God.

Conclusion:

Israel complains that God isn't aware of their trials and doesn't pay attention to their case. Isaiah answers that God has to be mindful because that is the very nature of God. In fact, the prophet shows them that God goes beyond the mere things that they ask. He provides strength to rise above the things they would desire removed, but the secret lies in "waiting" on the Lord.

Blessed Assurance
Isaiah 41:1–14

Introduction:
The song writer said, "If we could see beyond today." If we could, we would be prophets. Isaiah could see down the future, and he speaks as if Judah were already in captivity.

I. **The Problem**
    A. Describe the captivity period.
    B. Opposition is identified (vv. 11–12).
        1. Incensed: glow, grow warm, blaze up.
        2. Strive: contest, chide, controvert.
        3. Contend: quarrel.
        4. War: battle, fighting, warfare.
    C. Opposition interpreted—we face it too.
        1. Circumstantial currents.
        2. Pressure, heavy labor, demanding work.
        3. Personal hostility and opposition.

II. **The Prohibition** (v. 10*a*)
    A. "Fear thou not."
        1. Simple statement: do not be afraid, dread.
        2. Very complete commandment.
            a. Of people (what they can do to you).
            b. Of circumstances (of what will happen).
            c. Of yourself (of whether you can win).
    B. "Be not dismayed."
        1. From word that means to look around in amazement—don't be confused.
        2. This is something stronger than fear.
            a. Not only "don't be afriad."
            b. Also, don't even let the problems you face confuse you.

III. **The Promise**
    A. God doesn't give them an empty prohibition.
    B. He backs the prohibition with a promise.
        1. His presence: "I am with thee."
        2. His person: "I am thy God."
        3. His provision.
            a. I will strengthen thee: establish.
            b. I will help thee: surround with aid.
            c. I will uphold thee: maintain, stay up.

4. His preference (vv. 8–9).
    a. You are God's special people.
    b. God always takes care of His own.
5. His power (vv. 11–12).
    a. Note what He will do to their enemies.
    b. They think they are something—He'll make them nothing.
C. The exhibition of God's promise (vv. 1–7).
    1. Speaks of choice of Cyrus.
    2. God is never surprised or caught short.

Conclusion:

In the face of the things we all face—few of which could compare to the captivity for intensity—we are given "blessed assurance."

As Floods to a Thirsty Soul
Isaiah 44:1–5

Introduction:
The last part of Isaiah is a roller coaster ride. God has told Israel of great judgment awaiting, but He can't seem to leave things on negative note. He comes back to promise them good things as well and uses the simile of water for God's blessing. Why that likeness?

I. **Water is common, abundant, and available.**
   A. So God illumines every soul.
      1. Gives basic belief in God.
      2. Shows men that way they should walk (Bible).
      3. Enables discernment of right/wrong.
      4. Leads to grace if men will follow.
   B. Christ lights every man (John 1:9).
   C. To those who struggle to do right, His assisting grace is never wanting.

II. **Water is indispensable to life.**
   A. No spiritual life can begin without God.
   B. No spiritual life can exist without God.
   C. We face evils too subtle and mighty to yield to any other force.
   D. Without water of His blessing, we cannot know life and the meaning of life.

III. **Water cleanses.**
   A. Only the blessing of God (grace) can cleanse the soul.
   B. Grace of God effectively deals with sin.
      1. Deals with the sin itself.
      2. Deals with the guilt of the sin.
      3. Deals with place where sin originates.
   C. There is no other effective remedy for sin.

IV. **Water renews and refreshes.**
   A. God provides spiritual renewal and refreshment.
   B. Renewal and refreshment bring change.
   C. The Spirit poured out it.
      1. The Lord's life.
      2. The Lord's light.
      3. The Lord's love.

V. Water gives life.
A. Absence of water normally means absence of life.
B. Only God's blessing gives life.
1. Man has constructed many ways.
2. Only God can get us back to God.
C. Without something supernatural, there is no possibility of life.

Conclusion:

God uses the simile of water for blessing for very good reasons:

Water is abundant and free—as His blessing.

Water is indispensable—as His blessing.

Water cleanses—as His blessing.

Water renews, refreshes—as His blessing.

Has He poured water on you? Have you declared your thirst?

Thy God Reigneth

Obadiah

Introduction:
Obadiah is the shortest book in the Old Testament. It doesn't deal directly with Jews, but rather it has to do with a nation named Edom.

I. **The Background of the Book**
  A. Descendants of Esau.
    1. Always hated Jacob (Gen. 27:40–41).
    2. Married heathen women.
  B. Showed hostility to Israel after the Exodus (Num. 20:14–21).
  C. Numbered among Israel's enemies by Saul (1 Sam. 14:47–48).
  D. David fought against them (1 Chronicles 18:11–13).
  E. Finally culminated in Edom's gladness over destruction of Jerusalem (Lam. 4:21–22).
  F. Nation was destroyed, but people were not (Herod was Idumean—Edomite).
  G. Time perspective—between destruction of Jerusalem and cir. 550 B.C.

II. **The Teaching of the Book**
  A. Introduction (v. 1).
  B. The warning to Edom (vv. 2–9).
    1. They thought selves secure/safe.
    2. Assured that such would not deter God's intentions for them.
  C. The reason for Edom's judgment (vv. 10–14).
    1. Refers to destruction of Jerusalem in 586 B.C.
    2. Edom had no real part in that.
    3. They had rejoiced and made no effort of any kind to help.
  D. The judgment on Edom (vv. 15–21).
    1. "Day of the Lord" coming.
    2. Israel will totally overcome and possess them in day of kingdom.

III. **The Implications of the Book**
  A. God deals with the nations on the basis of their relationship to His people.

     1. United States does not equal Old Testament Israel.
       a. Much confusion caused by this.
       b. Some "promises" questionable.
     2. The "church which is His body" is equivalent today.
B. God deals with Edom more for its spirit than for its actions.
     1. No evidence it participated in sack of Jerusalem.
     2. Singled out for attitude of heart (note vv. 12–14) .
     3. Sounds a note of warning to us.
       a. Proverbs 3:27
       b. Proverbs 24:17–18
       c. Proverbs 24:11–12

Conclusion:

Edom was facing judgment. The sin of Edom was a vengeful, hateful spirit. Hear God's message to us: Stay out of God's business, and get into your own business.

Not to Worry!

Matthew 6:25–34

Introduction:

Worry and fear are closely akin; but worry is much more common than fear, needs far less basis than fear, and tends to be more all-consuming (we are afraid at times but worry all the time). God's Word speaks very clearly about worry in several places.

I. **A Prohibition**

"Take no thought" (vv. 25, 31, 34).

A. Obviously does not mean what it says:
1. We are commanded several places to give thought to the future.
2. Believe it is right to consider the cost before plunging into something.
B. It must—and does—have another meaning.
1. Idea is "be not anxious."
2. This is a direct and specifiç prohibition of worry in all its forms (even "concern").

II. **Some Principles**

God doesn't just tell us not to worry; He gives us good reason to obey that prohibition.

A. Don't worry—it is unnecessary for the children of such a father. (vv. 25b–30)
1. He has already given you life and body—won't He give you the rest? (v. 25b)
2. He cares for the creature world—not for you? (v. 26)
3. Why engage in the needless?—worry is totally non-productive. (v. 27)
4. He cares for the temporary—not for the immortal? (vv. 28–30)
B. Don't worry—it is unworthy the subjects of such a kingdom. (vv. 31–33)
1. This is what preoccupies the minds of the heathen—yours too? (v. 32a)
2. When you worry, you intrude into the area of the Father ("Let me worry about that"). (v. 33b)
3. You have many other things to be concerned with instead of wasting time on this. (v. 33)
4. Might as well as be working as sitting around worrying. (v. 33)

C. Don't worry—it is unfruitful. (v. 34)
1. Don't worry about tomorrow, you can only live today.
2. Don't worry about tomorrow, it will have its own supply of problems you haven't even thought about yet.
3. Don't worry about tomorrow, it will bring its fresh supply of strength ("as thy days, so shall thy strength be").

III. The Practicalities

Worry is usually an indication of:
A. Unwillingness to trust the promises of God.
1. He has promised to supply every need.
2. My worry is indication that I don't believe He can or will do so.
B. A sense of unworthiness to have my needs supplied.
1. Usually stems from guilt over something I have done or am doing.
2. Goes back to unwillingness to trust the promises because all is covered by them.
C. A lack of surrender to the will of God.
1. Sometimes we know that God can and will supply our need but still worry.
2. Problem is that we are not sure He will do it the way or to the extent we wish.
3. Worry is one of the signs of an unsurrendered will.

Conclusion:

We won't do much about worry until we begin to recognize the underlying cause. We can know freedom from worry when we come to terms with what God is trying to do in our lives.

Digging Deep When Times Are Good

Matthew 7:24–27

Introduction:
This story is most familiar, but there is a lesson each of us needs in order to handle the inevitable difficulties of life.

I. **The Story**
    A. Two men (probably little outside difference between them).
    B. Two houses (may have also been very similar).
    C. Two foundations (extremely dissimilar).
    D. One storm.
    E. Two results.
        1. One house stood firm (may have been damaged, etc.).
        2. Other house was demolished.

II. **The Lessons to Be Learned from It**
    A. The storms will come!
        1. Trials
        2. Physical/mental afflictions
        3. Circumstances
        4. Persecution
        5. Satanic suggestions, temptations, insinuations
        6. Doubt, despondency, despair, depression
        7. Misunderstanding
    B. The foundation determines the staying power.
        1. No indication anything different about houses.
        2. The whole difference was in the foundation or lack of one.
    C. The foundation must be built before the storm breaks.
        1. It requires sincere effort.
        2. It involves expenditure of time.

III. **The Action to Be Taken**
    A. Stablish the relationship.
        1. Father-child relationship
        2. Family relationship—are you part of the family?
    B. Settle the issues.
        1. God's character
        2. God's sovereignty
        3. God's providence (another way of expressing Rom. 8:28)

C. Submit to the will of God.
　　1. You can trust a God like the One we know.
　　2. Can't change His will anyhow.
D. Strengthen the walk.
　　1. Make the Word part of life.
　　2. Become familiar with prayer.
　　3. Make obedience primary.
　　4. Seek to overcome sin.

Conclusion:

The storms hit everyone, including Christians. Some survive; some are devoured. The only way to withstand the storm is dig the foundation and to do so before the storm. The foundation begins with a personal relationship to Jesus Christ. Have you taken that step? Make work of digging deep when times are good.

Master, the Tempest Is Raging

Matthew 8:23–27

Introduction:

This very familiar story about the disciples in the storm not only gave rise to the familiar gospel song, but it also teaches us lessons about the experiences common to everyday life.

I. **The Nature of the Storm**
    A. Explain location of sea and mountains.
    B. Characteristics of storm.
        1. Sudden
        2. Unexpected
        3. Fierce
            a. Waves breaking over boat.
            b. Boat filled with water.
            c. Remember, these were sailors.
    C. Similitude: a parable of life.
        1. Storms come.
        2. Possess similar qualities.
        3. Speaks to all our lives.

II. **The Message of the Storm**
    A. It speaks of human frailty.
        1. They were overwhelmed.
        2. They were terrified.
    B. It speaks of human inadequacy.
        1. There was nothing they could do.
        2. They were at the mercy of the storm.
    C. It speaks of human faithlessness.
        1. They did seek the Lord's help.
        2. They were very perturbed with Him.
        3. "Carest thou not that we perish?"
        4. They were rebuked on this score.

III. **The Silence of the Storm**
    A. It says nothing about His presence.
        1. The facts:
            a. They were in His will.
            b. He was present with them.
        2. The meaning:
            a. Storms say nothing about His will or presence.
            b. He is always present with us in the storm.
    B. It says nothing about His concern.

1. The facts:
    a. They question because He sleeps.
    b. His concern obvious with thought (He would have gone down with them had the ship sunk).
2. The meaning:
    a. His care is sure (Matt. 6:25–34).
    b. His silence does not indicate unconcern.
C. It says nothing about His ability.
    1. The facts:
        a. Even nature obeys His command (because He is Creator).
        b. He willed the peace (words for the sake of the disciples).
    2. The meaning:
        a. Options here: was not time yet; would not have gone down; storm would have ceased.
        b. Either He keeps us through the storm, stops the storm, or takes us out of the storm.

Conclusion:

The storms of life come and show us what we really are, but the storms say nothing about crucial issues. Are you in the storm? God is with you, He is concerned about you; and He will either keep you through the storm, stop the storm, or take you out of the storm. The need is for faith.

Assurances in the Storm

Matthew 14:22–32

Introduction:

Christ had just fed the five thousand and sent His disciples across the lake while He went to pray. They got into a storm, just as we are often in a storm. Here as some assurances:

I. **He brought me here.**
   A. You can get into a storm while right in the center of God's will.
      1. They were doing what He had directed.
      2. Problems are not sure sign of His displeasure.
   B. There is a purpose to our being in the storm.
      1. Sometimes puts in storm to keep from sinning.
      2. Sometimes puts in storm to prepare for new ministry.
      3. Sometimes puts us in storm to draw us closer to Him and each other.

II. **He is mindful of me.**
   A. Christ knew where they were and what was going on.
   B. His prayer (v. 23) doubtlessly included them.
      1. Moses on mountain praying for Israel.
      2. Christ on mountain praying for disciples.

III. **He will come to me.**
   A. If you feel deserted:
      1. God comes at darkest hours to teach us not to depend on circumstances.
      2. Storms are never pleasant experiences unless safety is sure.
   B. Storms are often preludes to miracles.
   C. Thing that frightens you is often Christ's way of coming nearer to you (He will use the vehicle of the storm).

IV. **He will help me grow.**
   A. Christ tries to teach us to trust Him—Peter got the idea.
   B. Peter's walk on the water in the storm and in the dark with his eyes on Jesus defines the Christian life.
      1. He sank because He got his eyes off the Lord.
      2. Don't criticize Peter—he had a word and walked on water; we have a whole Bible and can't walk on the sidewalk.

C. Lessons to be learned from Peter's failure.
   1. Obstacles are what you see when you get your eyes off Jesus.
   2. We don't enjoy the storms, but God employs the storms.

V. He will see me through.
A. Faith remembers the promise: He told them, "I'll see you on the other side." They *had* to get there.
B. He will bring you out of the storm.
   1. You will get to know Him better and better.
   2. Keep your eyes on Him in the Word.
   3. You *will* reach the shore.

Conclusion:
We are in a storm. God brought us here, He knows we are here, He will come to us, and He will see us through. But He wants us to grow in the storm.

Walking on Water

Matthew 14:22–36

Introduction:
Faith is a strange thing! Most of us have enough to trust Jesus to keep us out of hell and get us into heaven, but few of us have enough to trust God to keep us day by day and see us through the tough times.

I. **The Storm in His Will**
    A. They had done what Christ told them to do (v. 22).
        1. Get in a boat and go to the other side.
        2. So they were clearly in His will.
    B. They kept on going because told to do so (v. 24).
        1. Could have solved problem by "running with the wind."
        2. Wouldn't because of obedience.
    C. We can be in the storm in God's will.
        1. Storm no sure sign out of His will.
        2. The will of God is likely to involve storms.
    D. Better stay in the storm in His will.
        1. Storm no reason to change direction.
        2. Doing so would have cost them a blessing.

II. **The Security of His Watchfulness**
    A. Christ was not present (v. 23).
        1. He sent multitudes away.
        2. Then withdrew to pray.
    B. Christ knew their situation.
        1. His knowledge was not based on His physical presence.
        2. Now His unlimited presence assures of complete knowledge.
    C. Christ went unto them.
        1. He was actually always with them.
        2. He went the way that they had gone (v. 25).
        3. He went to meet their need.
    D. Christ startled them.
        1. His coming caused them fear.
        2. Sometimes in the storm the thing that causes us the most fear is the vehicle of His coming.

III. **The Walk on the Water**
   A. It was not a presumptuous act.
      1. No command of God ever involves presumption.
      2. If Peter's request had been wrong, Christ's response would have been different.
   B. It was marred by an inadequate faith (v. 30).
      1. Peter centered on circumstances.
      2. Took his eyes off Jesus to look at the wind.
   C. It was a demonstration of remarkable faith.
      1. Don't criticize Peter.
      2. Most of us have never been out of the boat.
   D. It was a classic example of obedient faith.
      1. When Jesus says, "Come," we must go.
      2. So long as we center on Him we cannot fall.

Conclusion:

Are you in the storm? Jesus knows where you are and will come to you. Have you failed to get out of the boat when He said, "Come"? Come on out of the boat and take the steps of faith. He didn't let Peter go down. He won't let you down.

When the Storms of Life Overtake You

Matthew 14:22–36; Mark 4:35–41

Introduction:
Life is sufficiently turbulent to be well compared to a storm. The wind blows, the rain falls, and the elements rage.

I. **The Certainty of the Storms**
   A. All of us face them.
   B. Much worse for some.
   C. Much worse for some than for others.
   D. Come in so many forms.
      1. Money runs out.
      2. Lose a loved one.
      3. Problems at work.
      4. Depression.
      5. Marriage problems.
      6. Disappointing child.
      7. Failure in some endeavor.
      8. Emotional upset.

II. **The Assurance in the Storm**
   A. God will take you out of the storm.
      1. Paul at Ephesus.
      2. In His good time.
   B. God will make the storm stop.
      1. Disciples in boat.
      2. Very often happens.
   C. God will see you through the storm.
      1. He knows where you are.
      2. He is present even though unseen.
      3. He knows how much you can handle.
         a. Has promised not to give too much.
         b. Is honor bound to intervene.
         c. No boat He was ever in sank.
      4. He won't let you be overwhelmed.
         a. Storm can get pretty wild (Luke 8:23).
         b. He cares and can stop storm at will.
         c. You can only be overwhelmed by choice.
      5. He wants to show Himself to and for you.
         a. Storm often gives Him opportunity.
         b. Peter wouldn't have missed that one.

6. He wants you to grow.
    a. We often grow through trials.
    b. Can't get strong without pressure.
7. He wants to do some miracles.
    a. Disciples got two here—at least.
    b. Storms often launch-pads of miracles.
8. You are not necessarily out of His will (Matt. 14:22).
9. You are to exercise faith in the storm (Matt. 8:26).
    a. Rebukes came because of failure of faith.
    b. All other factors should make faith easier.
10. When you get through the storm you'll love Him more (Matt. 8:27).
    a. True of individual storms.
    b. True of life in general.

III. Our Approach to the Storm
A. Accept the real facts as they are.
B. Trust Him completely.
C. Stay where you are—let Him move you.
D. Get to know Him better—by knowing His Word.
E. Refuse to panic.
F. Expect Him to do great things.

Conclusion:
When the storms of life overtake you, praise the Lord!

The Focus of Faith

Matthew 14:23–33; Mark 6:45–52; John 6:16–21

Introduction:

One doesn't need to be a perfectionist for some things to bother him. A car that idles rough, a singer who doesn't stay on key, or pictures shown out of focus can all irritate. We like things fine tuned, and it seems that this miracle was designed to fine-tune or focus faith. . .

I. **On Direction, Not on Difficulties**
   A. They were doing His will—"constrained" (Matt. 14:22).
      1. To get people to leave.
      2. Didn't want to go without Him.
      3. Didn't want to leave Him alone.
      4. Didn't want to miss show (John 6:15).
   B. They were facing great difficulty.
      1. Making no progress against wind.
      2. They were "toiling" (Mark 6:48).
   C. Problems no sure sign regarding His will.
      1. Message of storm: "examine yourself."
         a. Jonah too dominant in our thinking.
         b. Look to Paul in trouble.
      2. Be sure of His will.
         a. In conformity to Word?
         b. Expect problems in His will.

II. **On His Person, Not on His Presence**
   A. He went to the mountain to pray; they went to the sea to row.
   B. They had a previous experience.
      1. He stilled the storm.
      2. He was in the ship with them.
      3. Now they were alone.
   C. He "saw them" (Mark 6:48). *Who* He is always more important than *where* He is.
   D. Once prayed for His presence; now pray for awareness of His presence.
      1. "Lo, I am with you always" (Matt. 28:20).
      2. "I will never leave thee nor forsake" (Heb. 13:5).
   E. Concentrate on Him at all times regardless of how things may seem.

III. **On Assurances, Not on Appearances**
   A. Three problems in appearance.
      1. Seemed He would never come (4th watch).
      2. Manner in which He came (on water).
      3. He made as if to pass by (Mark 6:48).
   B. Realities.
      1. Christ never comes late (Psalm 46:5).
      2. Form in which He comes unexpected.
      3. He appears to bypass.
   C. Must rest on assurances not appearances.
      1. Had seen much and already forgotten.
      2. We quickly forget and focus on things that appear.
      3. Need to concentrate on assurances (His promises and previous works).

IV. **On Completion, Not on Circumstances**
   A. As He entered, ship at shore (John 6:21).
      1. Not likely another miracle.
      2. He alleviated circumstances which made completion possible.
   B. Need to focus on completion of task, not on intervening circumstances.
   C. If the matter is in God's will.
      1. Forget the circumstances.
      2. Refuse to stop short of completion.

Conclusion:
We are to walk by faith. If we are ever going to be successful in doing so, we had better fine-tune the focus of our faith: on direction, not on difficulties; on His person, not His presence; on assurance, not on appearances; on completion, not on circumstances. Is your faith in His person in the first place?

Philip: Let's Hear It for the Common Man

John 1:43–46

Introduction:

When we list the disciples, we tend to run out at number nine or so. We know little about some whose names we do know. He had eternity's business to do in a short time and still selected some "no-names" to do His work. Philip is one of better known, but he's not distinguished, and he often appears overmatched by life. But the life of Philip holds hope for all of us.

I. **There is a place for the common man** (1:43–46).
    A. Jesus "found" him—all others came to Christ.
        1. Peter, great man; Andrew, man of initiative; Nathanael, man of spiritual depth; all come to Christ.
        2. Christ goes after Philip, ordinary man of limited abilities.
    B. Jesus invited Philip to follow—obvious that he did.
        1. First went and found Nathanael.
            a. Some indication they had been studying together.
            b. Nathanael's response problematic—may have had personal hang-up on Nazareth. ("Nathanael uses intelligent human observations to set a firm limit on the power of God, a process intelligent humans have been repeating all too often ever since.")
        2. Philip didn't know answer—just said, "Come and see" (v. 39).
            a. Note order—come and then see.
            b. Not necessary to know all answers to render service.
    C. Philip shows God has place and use for ordinary people.

II. **There is help for "little faith"** (6:5–7).
    A. Christ asks Philip where to get bread (don't know why Philip).
        1. Question designed to test Philip.
        2. Philip sounding board on which weaknesses of entire group sounded out.
    B. Philip could see the problem but not how to solve it.
        1. Had failed to learn lesson of what Christ had already done.

2. Missed point of what Christ would do and could do.
3. Balked at Christ repeating something already done (so do we).
C. Philip shows that Christ doesn't give up on "little faith."

III. **There is help for uncertainty** (12:20–22).
A. Greeks come to Philip seeking Jesus.
1. Review who they were.
2. They obviously wanted an interview with Him.
B. Philip didn't know what to do with their question.
1. Ministry of Christ up to then entirely in Jewish context.
2. Philip faced with great dilemma so threw it to Andrew.
C. Philip shows that God is patient with our uncertainty.

IV. **There is a solution for the one dimensional** (14:7–10).
A. Philip interrupts Christ's teaching.
1. Christ teaching Thomas.
2. Something comes up that Philip doesn't understand.
3. Philip blurts out interruption.
B. Philip's problem is believing what he couldn't see.
1. "Show" us the Father, then we can believe.
2. Very common problem for us—we can easily believe what we can see, but we balk at the invisible.
C. Philip shows that God wants us to move beyond the "one-dimensional" level where we usually live.

Conclusion:

Philip was just an ordinary man, but Christ still sought him and made him part of His disciple band. This teaches us that God is more patient than we are, and ordinary people like Philip demonstrate that God has a place for ordinary people.

Surprise! Surprise! Surprise!

John 1:45–51

Introduction:

Gomer Pyle said it so many times that it became a byword, but Nathanael experienced it long before Gomer was invented. When he came to Jesus, he found surprises galore, and there were three that are notable.

I. **He was surprised by joy** (vv. 45–46).
    A. Appears to be serious, dour, straight-laced, narrow.
        1. May be revealed in question "Can any good thing come out of Nazareth?"
        2. May have been tied to higher expectation.
        3. May have involved fact Galilee was tainted by Gentile contact.
    B. Not sure of what he sought; sure of what he found.
        1. Found a Christ of joy.
            a. Wedding reception.
            b. Picnic after service in a field.
            c. Banquet for converted tax collector.
            d. The ultimate buffet at Mary and Martha's.
            e. Even last supper was a supper.
        2. He was surprised by joy.
    C. The Christ we proclaim is a Christ of joy—where is yours?

II. **He was surprised by righteousness** (vv. 47–48).
    A. Christ paid him high compliment.
        1. "Guile" has dual meaning that merges.
            a. Without hypocrisy (word used to describe Jacob in Greek translation—nothing of Jacob in him).
            b. Gentle, without intent to do harm.
        2. Christ commends him for his spiritual attainments.
    B. He appears to accept that compliment.
        1. Evidently agrees with assessment.
        2. Obvious from rest of story that there is something more.
    C. The righteousness we may have is not adequate—"To attain heaven by self-effort must remain forever an impossible dream."
        1. We are likely to be Nathanaels.
        2. We need the surprise of His righteousness that makes our own insignificant.

III. He was surprised by enlargement (vv. 48–51).
    A. Nathanael was not a big man.
        1. He was no doubt narrow and straightened in his religion.
        2. Evidently he was rather gullible.
           a. Jesus reveals a fact from before their meeting.
           b. He is so impressed that he immediately believes.
        3. Jesus appears to rebuke him for his shallowness (v. 50).
    B. He is surprised by the enlargement Jesus brings (v. 51).
        1. Is promised experience of far better things.
        2. Concourse between heaven and earth.
        3. Obviously involves miracles.
        4. All activity centers on Christ.
    C. He wants to surprise us with enlargement.
        1. We live in narrow little worlds and are gullible.
        2. He wants to do special things in our lives.

Conclusion:
Christianity and the Christian life are full of surprises! God wants to surprise us with joy, God wants to surprise us with the scope of His righteousness, and God wants to surprise us with enlargement. God wants you and me to know the real joy of living, a righteousness that is sufficient, and a relief from the routine and humdrum of daily life. Let God surprise you!

Need and Feed

John 6:1–15

Introduction:

Spurgeon said, "Our blessed Master, now that He has ascended into the heavens, has more rather than less power; He is not baffled because of our lack, but can even now use paltry means to accomplish His own glorious purposes."

I. **An Overwhelming Need**
   A. A vast multitude was present.
   B. They had walked/rowed significant distance to be there.
   C. They had given no thought to supplies.
   D. It was getting to be late in the day.
   E. They were hungry—can produce hardship (women, children there).

II. **A Discouraging Inadequacy**
   A. Christ's question points out their inadequacy (v. 5).
      1. Was designed to "test" him—draw out where he really was.
      2. Points out:
         a. No food.
         b. No money to buy food (year's wages for mere taste).
         c. No place to buy food even if money available.
   B. Christ's command makes inadequacy personal (Matt. 14:16—"Give ye them to eat.").
      1. Forces issue on them to show them how inadequate they really were.
      2. They were good at calculating, but not good at believing.
   C. Arrival of lad's lunch makes inadequacy even clearer (v. 9, ". . . but what are they among so many?").

III. **A Controlling Commitment**
   A. Christ commands them to sit in organized groupings.
      1. Word for recline to eat.
      2. People sit, thanks offered before provision made.
   B. Christ takes what is available and performs the miracle.
      1. Reminds us of Moses, "What is that in thine hand?"
      2. Note miracle of transformation (came to transform rather than create—water to wine; bread to more bread).

C. Christ is given:
1. Their unquestioned obedience.
2. Their meager resources. ("Anything that you take away from self and give to Christ is well invested.")

IV. An Abounding Provision
A. Don't know when or how of miracle.
1. No doubt as He broke and distributed.
2. The supply came as the need was being met (God often works that way).
B. He multiplied what they already had rather than providing something new.
1. It is Christ who provides for us, and we must be open to receiving it the way He chooses to provide for us.
2. "Christ is never in need but that He has somebody at hand to supply that need."
C. There was an abundance of supply.
1. They were all filled—had all they could ask for.
2. Picked up pieces and fragments, not scraps or crumbs.
3. Twelve baskets—each disciple had a basket to return.
4. There is much more left when they are finished then there was when they began.

Conclusion:
We live in needy world, and we are completely inadequate for most needs we meet. He is totally adequate for every need. It is often Christ's way to do that for His people of which there is no probability or likelihood that His glory may be seen the more brightly.

The Most Searching Question

John 21:15–17

Introduction:

Peter had blown it; in fact, he had blasted it away and done it in front of the other disciples. Three times he had denied even knowing Christ and that after having declared that denial was the one sin he would never commit. They had been together several times, and nothing had been said, but then it came— "Simon, Son of Jonas." But it wasn't what he had expected! Instead of a reprimand and rebuke, it was a simple question: "Lovest thou me more than these?"

I. **The Nature of the Question**
    A. Question instead of rebuke.
        1. Notice Christ's tenderness.
        2. If Peter's love for the Lord was intact, all else was well.
    B. "More than these."
        1. Could have three meanings.
        2. No doubt refers back to his foolish statement.
        3. Note that Christ drops subject when Peter doesn't address it.
    C. Repeated three times.
        1. Surely answers to three-fold denial.
        2. Designed to serve notice of Peter's restoration.
    D. Dealt with real issue.
        1. Deals with what is within.
        2. Gets to the heart of our relationship with Him.
    E. The question is still valid—"Lovest **thou** me?"
        1. "But we haven't denied, betrayed the Lord."
        2. Really?

II. **The Answer to the Question**
    A. Peter's answer direct and face to face.
        1. "I love you."
        2. "You know I love you."
    B. Christ's answer significant.
        1. "If you love me, then get busy with what I have given you to do."
        2. Love meaningless unless shown.
    C. Our answer is three-fold.
        1. Obedience (John 14:15, 21, 23–24; 1 John 2:3–6).

2. Love the brethren (1 John 3:23; 4:7–11, 20–21; John 13:34; 15:12).
3. Concern for the lost (John 15:9–17—summary of all three).

III. The Challenge of the Question
A. Easy to give an answer.
1. Of course we love the Lord.
2. We tend to have very warm feelings toward Him.
B. We deal here with something deeper than feelings.
1. Involves relationship.
2. Involves resulting action.
C. The answer must be lived.
1. Is there obedience?
2. Is there love for the brethren?
3. Is there concern for the lost?

Conclusion:
Peter was restored, put back on track, but the question still haunts—"Lovest thou me?" What is your answer?